DATE DUE

Tom and the Two Handles

Tom
and the

An I CAN READ Book®

Two Handles

by Russell Hoban
Pictures by Lillian Hoban

Harper & Row, Publishers

I Can Read Book is a registered
trademark of Harper & Row, Publishers, Inc.
Tom and the Two Handles
Text copyright © 1965 by Russell C. Hoban
Pictures copyright © 1965 by Lillian Hoban
Printed in the United States of America.
For information address Harper & Row, Publishers, Inc.
10 East 53rd Street, New York, N.Y. 10022.
Library of Congress catalog card number: 65-11459
ISBN 0-06-022430-4
ISBN 0-06-022431-2 (lib. bdg.)
ISBN 0-06-444056-7 (pbk.)

For Ferd

"What's the matter?"

said Father to Tom.

"Look," said Tom.

"Kenny gave me a bloody nose."

"You and Kenny had a fight?"
said Father.

"Yes," said Tom.

"And he gave me a bloody nose.

But I'll get him next time.

I'll get him good."

"Now, Tom," said Father,

"you don't want to go around

feeling like that.

Kenny's your best friend, isn't he?"

"Yes," said Tom,

"and next time

I'll give him a bloody nose

and a black eye."

"Tom," said Father,
"there is more than one way
of looking at a thing.

A very wise man once said
that a problem is like a jug
with two handles."

"What do you mean?" asked Tom.

"Well," said Father,

"you can say that Kenny

gave you a bloody nose

and next time you'll get even.

You can pick up the problem

by that handle.

Or you can say

that you had a bad time

with your best friend,

but you'll make up

and be friends again.

That's the other handle."

"Kenny is my best friend,"

said Tom.

"Then, which handle

will you try?" asked Father.

"I'll try the second handle,"

said Tom.

"I'll make up with Kenny

and be friends again."

So Tom went to make up

with Kenny.

"Hello," said Tom to Kenny.

"Hello," said Kenny.

"I was just coming
to tell you that I'm sorry
I gave you a bloody nose."

"That's all right," said Tom.

16

"Every problem has two handles.

And we're best friends."

"That's right," said Kenny.

"And it isn't fair

for me to pick on you.

Because I'm stronger than you are."

17

"What makes you think
you're stronger than I am?"
asked Tom.

"Well, I am," said Kenny.

"You're not so strong," said Tom.

"I could give you a bloody nose
if we had another fight."

"Let's see you try it," said Kenny.

So they had another fight,

and Kenny gave Tom

another bloody nose.

Tom told Father about it.

Father said, "Weren't you going
to make up with Kenny
and be friends again?"

"I wanted to make up," said Tom.

"But we had another fight,

and I lost.

How can we be friends

if I keep losing?"

"Well," said Father,

"let's see if there is

more than one way

of looking at it."

"You mean, look for

the second handle again?"

asked Tom.

"That's right," said Father.

"All I know," said Tom,

"is that I lost

two fights in a row."

"Yes," said Father, "but think

of all the fights you win."

"When I had a fight with Dick

I won," said Tom.

"And I beat Charlie too."

"You see?" said Father.

"There's the second handle.

Sometimes you win,

and sometimes you lose.

You can't win them all."

"Why not?" asked Tom.

"That's just how it is,"

said Father.

"You can't win them all."

The next day Kenny said,

"I'm sorry I gave you

a bloody nose. again."

"That's all right," said Tom.

"Every problem has two handles.

We're best friends.

And you can't win them all."

"What do you mean,

I can't win them all?"

said Kenny.

"Do you want to try it again?"

"All right," said Tom.

27

So they had another fight.

And Kenny gave Tom

another bloody nose.

"That's three in a row,"
said Tom to Father that evening.
"I don't know why you want
to keep fighting with Kenny,"
said Father.
"I don't want to," said Tom.
"But we keep fighting,
and I keep losing."

"Well," said Father,

"maybe it's time

to call a spade a spade."

"How many handles

does a spade have?"

asked Tom.

"Just one," said Father.

"I think maybe Kenny

is a better fighter than you are."

"Why is Kenny a better fighter?"

asked Tom.

"Show me how you fight,"
said Father.
Tom showed him.

"Well," said Father,

"you're not using your left hand right.

You have to stick it out

in front, like this."

And he showed Tom.

"But the best thing to do,"

said Father,

"is to make up with Kenny.

Be friends again."

"I'll try," said Tom.

The next day

Tom said to Kenny,

"Let's not fight anymore.

Every problem has two handles.

We're best friends.

You can't win them all.

And I don't use

my left hand right."

"You don't use

your right hand right, either,"

said Kenny.

"You're just not a very good fighter."

"Yes, I am," said Tom.

"No, you're not," said Kenny.

"I'll show you," said Tom.

So they had another fight.

And Kenny gave Tom

another bloody nose.

"Kenny," said Tom,

"I don't think

you're a very good best friend.

I've had four bloody noses

in a row from you."

"Who wants to be best friends
with you anyhow?" said Kenny.
And they both went home.

39

"Four," said Tom
to Father that evening.
"Four bloody noses from Kenny.
And I told him I didn't want
to fight anymore, too."

"Maybe you should find
somebody else to play with,"
said Father.

"Kenny was all right until
he started winning all the time,"
said Tom.

"And I think he would be

all right again

if I started winning

some of the time.

I think he should take turns losing.

What do you do

with your right hand

when your left hand

is sticking out the way

you showed me?"

"You keep it ready like this,"
said Father.

"Then you let it go like this."

And he showed Tom.

"You have to practice
to do it right," Father said.
"Practice makes perfect.
But that is not the way
to make up with Kenny."

"Maybe making up

has more than one handle,"

said Tom.

And he went down to the basement.

In the basement he found

an empty burlap bag.

Tom filled the bag with dirt
and tied the top shut.
Then he hung the bag
from a tree branch.

Tom practiced hitting the bag
with his right hand.

He practiced hitting the bag
with his left hand.

Tom did not play with Kenny.

Every day after school
he practiced hitting the bag
with his right hand
and his left hand.

One evening Tom said to Father,

"I think I'm ready

to make up with Kenny."

"I'm glad to hear that,"

said Father.

"Old friends are the best friends."

The next day
Tom went to play with Kenny.
"I think we should be
best friends again," said Tom.
"So do I," said Kenny.
"I never did want
to stop being friends.
You were the one
who kept wanting to fight."
"Well," said Tom,
"every problem has two handles.
Old friends are the best friends.
You can't win them all.

It's time to call

a spade a spade.

Practice makes perfect."

"What do you mean?" asked Kenny.

"I mean I can fight better
than I used to," said Tom.

"I still don't think
you're a very good fighter,"
said Kenny.

"Well, I am," said Tom.

"But old friends are the best friends.
So let's be friends and not fight."

"No, you're not," said Kenny.

"Not an old friend?" asked Tom.

"Not a very good fighter," said Kenny.

"Yes, I am," said Tom.

"Show me," said Kenny.

And they had another fight.

That evening Father said to Tom,

"Did you make up with Kenny?"

"Yes," said Tom.

"Now we are best friends again. That two-handled-jug man was a very smart man."

"What do you mean?" asked Father.

"Well," said Tom,

"after I gave Kenny a bloody nose,

I knocked him down.

Then I sat on top of him.

And I told him

there was more than one way

of looking at it.

I told him that he could say

I gave him a bloody nose.

Or he could say

that he had a bad time

with his best friend

and we could make up.

So we made up.

That two-handled-jug man was smart."

"Yes," said Father, "he was."

"Do you think I will ever

be that smart?" asked Tom.

"I don't know," said Father,

"but I think you are

off to a very good start."

The End